Merry Christmas, Jesus!

this book belongs to _____

First printing: September 2004

© 2003. All rights reserved.

No part of this book may be used or reproduced in any manner whatsoever without express written permission of the publisher except in the case of brief quotations in articles and reviews. For information write *Journey Stone Creations, LLC, 3533 Danbury Road, Fairfield, OH 45014*

ISBN Number: *0-9758709-6-3*

Printed in China through GlobalPSD

Please visit our web site for other great titles.

www.journeystonecreations.com

For information requesting author/illustrator interviews, please contact us at 513-860-5616 or e-mail *Pat@journeystonecreations.com; Suz@journeystonecreations.com*

the A.W.A. gang

ANGELS WITH ATTITUDES!

A PLACE FOR THE KING

The Christmas Story From The Angels' Point of View

Written By Patricia Stirnkorb

Illustrated By Suzanne Bock

The nine members of the A.W.A. Gang were playing at Paradise Park in Heaven, discussing the atmosphere of the day. They were all in agreement that something exciting was about to happen. James, the Archangel, and the one that passes out assignments to the Earth Angels, walked up to the kids.

"Hello Gang! How are you this wonderful day?" James asked. His glistening white robe seemed to have a bit more shine to it. And as one of the tallest of all the angels, he even seemed to stand a bit taller today.

"We're fine, James. But, what's up? It seems everyone is excited. Is something big about to happen?" Patrick, self-appointed leader of the Angels with Attitudes, asked.

"That's exactly what I am here to discuss with you. You see, before I can tell you what will happen now, I must take you back to a long, long time ago. For this assignment, you will remain in your heavenly robes and be invisible to humans on earth. That means you won't be able to interact with them at all," James explained. This was the first time the A.W.A. Gang received instructions like that.

"Wow! How come?" Patrick asked.

"To accomplish your next assignment, you will need heavenly wisdom and angelic powers. This is a very important assignment, and one the adult Earth Angels feel you are all ready to accomplish. Are you ready?" James asked.

"We're always ready for a new assignment!" said Andy. "I'll race you to the stairs!" Andy could always be counted on to spout out his opinion, whether anyone was interested in hearing it or not.

4

As the A.W.A. Gang headed for the golden stairway, James removed the sign that read "Do Not Slide on Banister."

"Got your Journey Stones? You'll need those to get you back here," he asked.

In unison the angels answered:

"Yes sir! Halos, Little lights, wings and stars. And of course our Journey Stones."

James watched as each member of the A.W.A. Gang climbed on the golden banister and slid to earth yelling "Angels Away!" as they disappeared from sight. Behind James, a bright light was glowing. He turned, and nodded in the direction of the light.

"They're off!" he said, smiling.

The nine angels that make up the A.W.A. Gang were recruited when heaven needed some extra Earth Angels to help accomplish all of the many tasks that needed to be done. When they heard some adult angels discussing the shortage of Earth Angels, they pleaded with the adults to allow them to be a part of the Earth Angel Force. Reluctantly, the adult angels agreed, giving their charge to James, the Archangel in charge of the E.A.F. It didn't take long for the adult Earth Angels to see what a great decision it was to include the A.W.A. Gang.

nce arriving on earth, Patrick removed the scroll of instructions from his backpack and the Gang gathered around while he read the message.

"*God has decided to send His only Son to be born on earth. It is your responsibility to find a place for the King of Kings to be born. Good luck!*" Patrick said.

As Kevin pulled his hand bells from his robe pocket, he began to sing.

"Wow! That's enough to make you want to sing! Hark! The Herald Angels Sing! Glory to the newborn King!" he bellowed at the top of his lungs.

"We are so lucky!" Chrisy said. "Can you imagine? We have been selected to find a place for the King of Kings to be born! What an awesome responsibility!"

"Yeah, I guess so," said Andy impatiently, "Let's get going. James said we didn't have much time."

As Bonnie skated ahead, Exxie ran beside her trying to keep up. They looked from side to side searching for something, although neither knew exactly what they were supposed to find.

"This place sure is big!" Exxie said. "Look at all the buildings. And the people dress funny. I wonder where we are…"

"I think this is the Roman Empire," said Bonnie. "Julius Caesar is in power. See the chariots?"

The A.W.A. Gang jumped to the side as three chariots whizzed past them.

"Hey! Watch it!" shouted Andy, waving his arms in the air as the chariots passed. "Are you blind or something?"

"Oh Andy! Remember James said we would be invisible to the people on earth. They can't see us." Anne said, coming up from behind with Kevin and Ray.

The A.W.A. Gang continued to walk until they saw a sign that read: "Palace This Way" pointing in the direction to the right of where they walked.

"That's it!" cried Ray, "A palace is what we need! James said it was for the King of Kings!"

"Great idea! Let's check it out," said Patrick.

As the Gang walked through the streets, people passed them without acknowledging their presence. They knew they were invisible. They decided to test out their speed factor and with the shout of "Angels Away!" they were transported to the front door of the palace.

"Do you think the guards can see us? Or can we just walk past them?" Thomas asked, hesitating at the edge of the walk that led to the palace door.

"No one else can see us. Let's go in and see what happens," said Kevin, in a slightly lower voice. The A.W.A. Gang walked in single file past the guards, who didn't even look in their direction.

Once inside the palace, the walls and ceilings were so big, the angels were amazed. The palace walls were decorated with gold, detailed statues, fountains, and beautiful flowers in vases as tall as Ray, the tallest of the A.W.A. Gang. Every kind of plant imaginable was growing inside this palace.

"What a wonderful place," said Patrick looking around in awe. "This is where the King of Kings should be born! What do you think, Gang?"

"I agree. Our work here is done," said Kevin. "Let's go back to Heaven and let James know we've found the perfect spot."

    "Yes, this assignment didn't take long," Chrisy said. "The King of Kings will have a place on earth almost as beautiful as Heaven."

    "Yeah! Let's get out of here," said Andy. "Being invisible is creepy. I keep thinking everyone is staring at me then I remember they can't see me at all!"

    The A.W.A. Gang each located their Journey Stones and held them firmly in their hands. With a nod from Patrick, they shouted "Angels Away" and instantly ...

... they found themselves back in Heaven, just as James was approaching them .

"Well, I see you've made it back. Any luck?" he asked.

"Oh yes!" exclaimed Patrick. "Wait until you see the glorious palace we found for the King of Kings. It has gold, and statues and flowers and fountains."

"It almost looks like Heaven!" said Andy.

"It is beautiful," said Ray. "We think the King of Kings will love His home."
But James wasn't so sure.

"A palace, hmmm… Angels, I don't think a palace is the right place. It might be big and beautiful, but well, this is for a Mighty Warrior.
He needs something different than
a palace..." James told the Gang.

"But you said it was for the King of Kings!" said Chrisy defensively. "We found a wonderful palace in Rome for the King of Kings."

"Oh, He is the King of Kings. But He is also a Mighty Warrior. Now you have to go back, and hurry. We don't have a lot of time."

"Back again? I sure hope we can find something this time," said Ray.

"I'll go back anytime," said Exxie. "I just love seeing all the sights! Let's go Bonnie!"

The Gang hurried back to the golden banister, hopped on and as they shouted "Angels Away!" they were gone in a blink.

T he A.W.A. Gang never knew where they would end up on the earth side of Heaven. But their assignment scroll from James always gave them an idea. This time they found themselves in a desert spotted with scraggly bushes and trees to the left, and to the right was a city in the distance. In front of them was a road sign that read "Jericho."

"Wow! I wonder where we are?" Patrick asked.

"Duh! Read the sign—It says Jericho." Andy said.

"Yes, I see that, but where is Jericho?" Patrick wondered.

"Well, do you remember our geography lessons?" Anne asked. "Jericho was a city in Israel. When the Israelites traveled around for those 40 years looking for the Promised Land, they sent spies into Jericho to check out the city."

"Spies! How exciting!" cried Kevin. "We're just like spies today! We're looking for something that needs to be found, and we're invisible to the people around us."

"I'd love to be a spy! Let's go see what we can find out!" said Exxie, heading up the hill towards the walls.

"Look at the walls. They are so thick people are walking on them. I bet this is a fort!" said Exxie.

"Actually, Jericho is a city. In the days of Moses, the Israelites surrounded the city and marched around it seven times. Then the walls came tumbling down. So we must be seeing this city before the walls fall," explained Chrisy.

"If the walls are going to fall, is this really the best place for a Mighty Warrior to be born? It could be dangerous, and at best, a temporary place for Him to live," Patrick said.

"You're right," said Ray. "Maybe we should keep looking..."

"I agree," said Exxie. "Let's find somewhere else to explore."

At the speed of light, the A.W.A. Gang was off again.

This time they found themselves in front of a castle. Guards were everywhere and the castle was surrounded by a moat filled with water.

"Now this is what I call a castle! Where are we?" asked Kevin.

"The sign says Judea, but I'm not sure," said Ray.

"Should we go in and check it out? Patrick, what does our scroll say this time?" Kevin asked.

Patrick removed the scroll from his backpack and began to read.

"'*The Son of God is also a Mighty Warrior. He will lead His people to victory and overcome evil.*' It sounds like this fort would be a great place," Patrick said.

"But when He is born, He's a tiny baby. Is this fort the right place for a new baby and His family to live?" asked Chrisy.

"How will we know if we don't stop talking about it and go check it out! Come on!" demanded Andy.

The A.W.A. Gang approached the castle hesitantly, and then Kevin began to sing at the top of his voice.

"There is sunshine in my soul today! More glorious and bright!" he bellowed.

"Hush!" hissed Andy. "What are you doing? You want everyone to see us coming? Remember, we are spies today!"

Kevin laughed at Andy. "Did you forget again Andy? No one can see us! We're invisible while we are on this assignment! I can sing as loud as I want!"

"So, I wonder if someone needed our help if we would be able to help them?" asked Thomas, lifting his First Aid kit in the air.

"I don't know Thomas, unless we are given immediate powers to appear to humans, I think our focus is on finding a spot for the King of Kings, the Mighty Warrior to be born," answered Anne.

"That's right, Gang. I'm sure glad I have my skates. This is a long road! Let's keep going," said Bonnie.

Once inside the castle, they saw hundreds of soldiers, all preparing for battle. Black smiths were working at fires, bows and arrows were piled high, and chariots and horses lined the stables along the walls. The inside of the castle was actually a military fort.

"Wow!" said Anne. "I've never seen so much equipment. Do you think they are getting ready for a battle?"

"I don't know, but let's keep looking. Remember, we need to think tiny baby. Is there a spot for Him here?" said Chrisy.

"Let's go this way, I see some buildings down at this end of the fort," said Thomas.

The A.W.A. Gang walked to the far side of the fort and found many smaller buildings where people lived. It was a city within the fort. There were shops selling food in the center of the town, a well to draw water from, and children playing in the streets. It looked like a normal city.

"There are lots of kids to play with," said Kevin. "And look, there are the women, cooking, and keeping house. This looks like a nice place. Then the Mighty Warrior could grow up knowing how to fight."

"Yes, it looks good to me. What do you think, Patrick?" Ray asked.

"It fits the description that James gave us this time. Let's get back to Heaven and see what he says," Patrick answered.

Huddling together, A.W.A. Gang reached in their pockets for their Journey Stones. Holding them tightly in their hands, they shouted, "Angels Away!" and instantly ...

...found themselves back in Paradise Park. James was approaching them.

"So, how did you do this time?" he asked expectantly.

"We told you we could handle the job," said Andy, sticking his chest out a little farther than normal. "We found a great fort for the Mighty Warrior, the King of Kings."

"A fort huh? Tell me about it," James said.

"It has lots of soldiers working on all different kinds of things," said Chrisy.

"Yes," said Exxie, "There are horses and chariots..."

"And kids playing in the streets. It's really more like a city within the walls. Like Jericho," explained Thomas.

"Even the walls are thick enough for men to walk on them, and they offer plenty of shelter from the outside world. The Baby would certainly be protected," said Ray.

"And He would grow up learning all the necessary tricks to being a soldier and a Mighty Warrior," said Patrick.

James listened closely to the A.W.A. Gang as they talked rapidly about their newest find.

"It sounds like you have certainly located a military fort. But I'm not sure that is the right place for God's Son to be born," said James. "After all, although He will be the King of Kings, and a Mighty Warrior, He is also the Lion of Judah... I think you may need to keep looking. But do it quickly, the time is drawing near."

"What? You mean, it's like, back to earth again?" asked Patrick surprised.

"That's right, and don't dilly dally. Time is running out. Now remember: Lion of Judah, King of Kings, Mighty Warrior," said James.

As the A.W.A. Gang headed for the banister, James looked over his shoulder and nodded towards the Light.

In unison the angels shouted, "Angels Away!" as they hopped upon the banister and headed back to earth.

They landed in a group of tall trees, covering the ground beneath them. It was soft, and dimly lit because the trees blocked out the sun. It was cool and very nice.

"Here we are! Look at these trees," said Patrick, staring at the tops of the trees all around them. "I've never seen anything so beautiful or so big!"

"Just listen to all the birds and animal sounds. This is a neat place," said Andy.

"I don't even care where we are!" said Exxie excitedly, " I want to stay here forever! I love it. And look, there's a snake!"

The rest of the A.W.A. Gang jumped aside as Exxie reached for the snake.
Just then something whizzed past her head.

"What was that?" Andy said. "A very big bug?"

"I don't know, maybe a bird. I think we're in a jungle," said Chrisy. "Maybe
in Africa or Ethiopia."

"It might be nice for you, but this soft ground keeps getting stuck in my
wheels. I can't get my skates going," said Bonnie. "Look there it is again...
What is it?"

A fast little something flew around the heads of the whole gang, as if checking them out. Suddenly it stopped right in front of Exxie's face.

"Look! It's a hummingbird! Hello there little fellow! Who are you?" Exxie asked.

The humming bird made a tiny sound, barely audible.

"Xavier?" asked Exxie. "What's a Xavier?"

"Not what's a Xavier, who's a Xavier. Me, I'm Xavier," the hummingbird answered.

"And you can talk?" asked Patrick in disbelief.

"All God's creatures can communicate," said Xavier. "It's just that people, and angels, don't always listen."

"Wow!" said Kevin. "That's enough to make me sing! Climb, climb up Sunshine Mountain! Heavenly faces glow.."

"Enough with the singing!" Andy shouted at him. " Let's just listen to the tunes of the birds! That's enough for me!"

Xavier giggled in a high-pitched, giddy voice.

The A.W.A. Gang began wandering off in different directions. It didn't take long for them to examine the different types of trees, the plants and to see lots of animals.

"This place is beautiful. Nature is all around us..." said Exxie, lifting her arms above her head and dancing from side to side.

"And heaven and nature sing! And heaven and nature sing! Joy to the world!" sang Kevin. "Come on, sing with me!"

Everyone ignored Kevin, who continued to sing. Andy rolled his eyes.

"But I'm not sure this is the place for a baby. It's dangerous," said Anne.

"Think of the adventures He will have!" coaxed Patrick. "Think of the fresh air and sunshine He'll get!"

"Think of the animals that could eat him in one bite! I don't think this is the place for the King of Kings," said Chrisy. "What do you think Xavier?"

"Bethlehem," said Xavier.

"Bethlehem?" asked Patrick. "What about Bethlehem? We've never even been to Bethlehem. I think we should go back to heaven and tell James what we found. Let God decide!"

As the angels reached for their Journey Stones, something else happened for the first time while the angels were on earth. James appeared in the midst of the Gang.

"Well, Gang, I see you found this quiet spot. Nice...But, not quite right for the King of Kings, the Mighty Warrior, the Lion of Judah," James explained. "It's really time to move along. I'm transporting you to Bethlehem, The King of Kings is about to be born. Get there quickly and search for the spot!"

"Bethlehem?" Patrick said, looking in the direction of Xavier. "Can you give us any idea of what to look for? All this about Mighty Warrior, Lion of Judah, King of Kings...isn't He just a baby?"

"He is indeed. The Lamb of the World. Now let's get moving! We're running out of time."

Almost as instantly as James and his glistening white robes disappeared, the Gang found themselves ...

... in the middle of a crowded street in Bethlehem. People were everywhere. Pushing and shoving, crowds of animals filled the streets; kids were running and shouting and street vendors were busy peddling their wares.

"Whoa! This sure is a busy place! Why don't we spread out and meet back here after we check out a few places?" said Ray. "This could take a while."

"Great idea! But we better hurry! James said we don't have much time," said Thomas. "Kevin, Chrisy, Anne and Exxie can come with me."

"And Bonnie, Andy, Ray and I will go in the other direction," Patrick said, in his take-charge voice. "But remember, James said time is running out. We have to hurry."

The Gang split up and went in two different directions.

"I've never seen so many people in one city. I wonder why they're all here?" asked Thomas.

"I don't know. There are signs all over that say 'Register here for taxes.' It must be time to pay their taxes to the government," replied Kevin.

"I overheard a man telling someone that everyone had to register in the town in which they were born. I guess a lot of people have been born here!" Chrisy added.

Anne hurried from behind and said, "Hey look! There's a big house, let's check it out and see if they have any room."

"I'll go ahead. I see some animals, and lots of little kids," Exxie said, hurrying off to see the animals all around.

The angels peered into the window of a house filled with adults and children. They were lying all over the floor with bedrolls. There were babies crying, mothers feeding little ones and other people trying to sleep. It looked like a giant slumber party! The gang traveled up and down the streets looking in windows and through open doors. Everywhere was crowded with people.

"Gosh! No place in there. We better keep looking," Exxie said.

"We could look forever! I wish we had a sign or something," said Chrisy. "How do you find a place for a baby King? I wonder if there is a palace here?"

"There are the others!" shouted Thomas. "I hope they've had more luck than us!"

The two groups joined together again, shaking their heads and talking low. There was just no available space in the whole city. Xavier, the humming bird, whizzed onto the scene, and gently landed on a sign that read "Inn--All Welcome." He bounced up and down a few times to get the Gang's attention.

"Look guys, Xavier is trying to tell us something! The sign! It's pointing to that big building. Let's go!" said Kevin.

The angels raced up the path to the Inn, just in time to see ...

... a man with a woman on a donkey. The man was talking to the Inn Keeper who was standing in front of an open door. The angels could see the place was packed with people. But they stood still and listened to the conversation.

"I'm sorry sir!" said the Inn Keeper. "We filled our last room just moments ago. I wish I could help you, but we have nothing left."

"I understand. But my wife is about to give birth. Do you know of anywhere that she can lie down and get some privacy?" the man asked.

The Inn Keeper's wife appeared at the door. He turned to her and asked, "What do you think about the stable? The cows are already in for the night, and so are the sheep and goats, but it is warm and quiet, and the straw would make a soft place to lie down."

" Of course! I'll get some blankets and some warm water to bathe with. I have some extra fruit and bread in the pantry," she said turning to get the things for the couple.

"Thank you so much. Mary is quite tired, and we've been traveling all day," the man replied, as they turned in the direction of the stable.

The angels listened with dismay and watched as the man and women headed for the stable.

"Great! We're too late again! I don't know what James expects us to do! There is no room in this whole city!" cried Andy, frustrated that they could not complete their assignment.

"There must be reason why James sent us here," remarked Patrick. "We must be missing something."

"Maybe it's to learn something about patience. Or how to be more creative when we think of what people on earth need. It's obvious they don't need a palace to have a baby, because that woman is about to have one in a barn!" said Bonnie.

The angels looked in the direction of the stable and watched as a star miraculously appeared over it. Suddenly, the sky was filled with angels! James, Michael, Gabriel, many others the Gang recognized. They were all wearing glistening robes unlike any the A.W.A. Gang had seen before! What was happening? What's going on, the Gang wondered. Just then, a group of shepherds raced towards the A.W.A. Gang.

"Excuse me! Have you seen the King? We've followed the star from our hillside, searching for the newborn king. The angels appeared to us and said to follow the star--that one! Where is the king?" a shepherd asked Patrick.

"King? I don't know. There is a man and his wife in the stable, under that star, but we haven't seen a king."

The shepherd looked in the direction of the barn and grabbed Andy's arm excitedly.

"Come with us, we'll find him together," he said.

"Hey! He can see us! We aren't invisible anymore! What is happening?" asked Andy.

Kevin couldn't take his eyes off the heavenly choir that had assembled above the stable. The music was beginning to fill the air.

"I don't know, but I'm going to go and sing with the other angels! I'll meet you later," he said, as he sped off to join the adult angels. Kevin took a spot near the end of the line and the sky was filled with spectacular music as the angels sang, looking down on a mother, father, and their newborn baby.

"Could this be the King? The Lamb of the World?" Chrisy asked, amazed at the scene before them.

"The Mighty Warrior?" Thomas asked.

"The King of Kings?" said Bonnie.

"The Lion of Judah?" Ray chimed.

Just then, James appeared in front of the Gang.

"This is the one who is called Christ Jesus. The Messiah, the King of Kings, the Mighty Warrior, Prince of Peace, Son of God, Son of Man, Lion of Judah, the Lamb of the World. He was sent to take away the sins of man kind. It is He, God's only Son," James said, glowing with a radiance the A.W.A. Gang could not explain.

"Wow!" Said Chrisy. "But we didn't find a place for Him, James. We didn't know what to expect."

"Don't worry, God had it under control. He sent Jesus to be a gift to man, but there was no place for him in the world. This place was chosen long ago," James explained.

"Then why did you send us out looking for a spot?" Andy asked.

"Because you needed to see for yourselves that the God of all creation sent His Son to live among men, humble enough to be born in a stable instead of a palace. This lesson will help you with your heavenly assignments," James explained.

All of the A.W.A. Gang stood watching as the tiny Baby reached for His mother's hand. Anne was the first to step forward and look at the Baby Jesus.

"Do you think He knows we're here?" she asked James.

"I'm sure of it. Just look at the way He is smiling at you," James replied.

The angelic choir continued to sing and the A.W.A. Gang heard Kevin calling and waving to them.

"Hey Gang! Look at me! I'm singing with the adult choir!" Kevin smiled and waved with one hand, ringing his bells with the other.

"And doing a fine job, Kevin!" shouted James. "Keep up the good work! You might have a future in music!" James laughed with the others.

"I still don't see why you wanted us to travel all around the world looking for a place that was never going to be good enough for this King," Thomas said.

James leaned a little closer to the kids as he told them.

"For thousands of years the world will reject this baby. His birth was predicted long ago, yet people still couldn't accept Him as their Savior. If He were born in a palace, or a fortress, or a jungle or an Inn, people would think of Him differently. He was born in a stable, to show He was humble enough to reach any one. He will one day rule the world; He will walk among man; and He will die for the people He loves," James said.

"And to think, we watched it all happen!" said Thomas.

"You were part of the plan," James said.

The angels stood looking at the baby, along with the shepherds, and the angels singing above them all.

"This is it gang, the perfect place for the king. It's the best place of all," Patrick said.

NOTE FROM THE AUTHOR AND ILLUSTRATOR:

We hope you have enjoyed reading about the A.W.A.Gang and want to learn more about their earthly adventures. Please watch for the following titles in this line:

In The Beginning...

Here Kitty

Big Bad Bully

Treasure Found

Meet the Angels

This Little Light

It is our desire that all children should know the story of God.

Parents, if your child or children have questions about God, Christ or Heaven after reading one of our books, please go to our web site at www.journeystonecreations.com and check out the Parents page. This helpful information will provide a way to discuss these topics with children.